I WANT TO GIVE YOU AN INCREDIBLE FREE GIFT

Over £500 Worth Of Powerful Tools & Resources To Free Your Business From The Exhausting Traps On Its Way To Customer Happiness.

**Just go to
www.noelcardona.com/opex**

OPERATIONAL EXCELLENCE FOR SUCCESSFUL CEOs

OPERATIONAL EXCELLENCE FOR SUCCESSFUL CEOs

By Noel Cardona

2018

First Printing: 2018

ISBN 978-0-244-07907-9

Noel Cardona Enterprises
www.noelcardona.com/opex

"Things may come to those who wait, but only the things left by those who hustle."

Abraham Lincoln

TABLE OF CONTENTS

INTRODUCTION

Thank you, and congratulations. Thank you, because if you value your time as much as I value mine, the minutes you are investing in studying what I have to teach you are precious. I will promise to try my best not to disappoint you.

I am an improvement professional who is an engineer by trade. I have worked in Production, Safety, Processes, Hygiene and Quality. With over 12 years of experience working with some of the best companies in two different continents, I have gained a unique vision of running companies towards operational excellence. This experience is what makes me qualified to share this knowledge with you. I have been on the battlefield; some battles were lost but many were won. Which battles, you may ask, and who have I been fighting against? Well, it turns out that I was at war not with just one enemy but with several. In each battle, I had to use five main weapons to defend and safeguard the single most important asset that such enemies wanted to capture: The trust our customers place upon us.

In this short book you will learn about the five weapons or, as I call them, the five pillars that I used, and still continue to use. You will also learn about the 10 main enemies that attempt to destroy your business on a daily basis without you realising it.

As a last note, although in this book I use war, enemies and fighting as a way to explain operational excellence, I do not support violence. The only justifiable conflict, from my point of view, is the one we all need to put ourselves through, such as self-analysis and corrective action, in order to improve our lives according to each individual's goals.

If you want to get an initial score to determine how strong your operations are, please go to the link below to download your "Operational Excellence Score" tool.

www.noelcardona.com/opex

BEGIN
WITH
THE END IN MIND

Before we even go into the subject of the five pillars, I would like you to think about the end goal for all the systems, all the effort and all the improvement work that is done at any organisation. What is that for? Have you forgotten? Have you been so lost in your day-to- day that you no longer remember who is paying your salary? Let me remind you: The one who pays your salary is not your boss or the shareholders of the business. They simply direct part of the money they receive to all employees. If there is no money to share, there is no business. Therefore, without customers, you don't have a salary. I know every single CEO reading this book knows that, I am not trying to patronise you. However, do you know why your customer gives you his or her money? Is it just in exchange for a product or a service? If you answered yes to the question above, you must review the very basics of your business knowledge. Customers hardly ever look for a single transaction, they look for businesses which they can trust, who offer what I call a Total Solution: **Before**, **during** and **after** they have paid you. What do I mean by that? Well, let's see. **Before** someone is your customer, that person is looking for somebody who can convince them that they will deliver on what it is being promised. This stage is critical because customer expectations are born at this point, creating a baseline which will be used to judge your performance during your relationship with them. Such expectations will come not only from what you tell them but also from what they see, and will have a tremendous impact on your price elasticity. Claire Rayner, in her book *The Retail Champion*, describes it very well as she talks about "The Arrows" for your business. She discusses the example of Ryanair, an economy airline that operates in Europe. Claire explains that the general look of Ryanair - The colours chosen for the plane, marketing and even uniforms - bring a sense of cheap services in-line with the actual prices charged. The best way I can summarise this is, as they say: Perception is reality. Therefore, how your customer perceives you and what you promise to them becomes their reality. Another way to view it would be to think about the implicit and explicit promises you are making to them.

Once your business has managed to turn that prospect into a customer, it is then that the explicit promises made before, which tend to be more general, become more specific. Here is where your customer starts holding you accountable via numbers such as dates, amounts, costs and other performance measures (the **"during"** stage). It is here where the trust we discussed starts to grow and to become an asset for your business. Trust never stops growing and is renewed every time you interact with your customers or clients. *Customer Trust is rented*: You have to pay the price continuously to keep that asset. By the way, trust is like a tree with shallow roots: It takes a long time to grow but can easily fall down and die.

Finally, **after** you have delivered the product or service, your customer has a much better picture in terms of promises vs reality and it will be an improved or worsened perception. For any customer, the transaction that just happened does not end there. During the whole sales process, your business made a promise which will not be delivered unless your customer needs to trigger it. That is the guarantee or risk reversal which is a ticket for your customer to request help, free of charge, because what you delivered didn't perform. This is the **"after"** stage. As counterintuitive as it is, more trust can be grown during this stage than in the other two combined. This is because you have demonstrated, in times of trouble, that you were there, took care of the situation, had the resources, and you made the process as easy and as inexpensive as possible for them (think money and time). You effectively became their superhero. Companies like Amazon or Zappos are well known for understanding this concept and for taking the opportunity to shine in times of hardship for their customer.

THE 10 ENEMIES YOU ARE AT WAR WITH

Let's first get to know our opponents so you know exactly where to aim the five weapons you will learn to use from this book.

THE BLINDFOLDED ARCHER
Your First Enemy

Remember the story of William Tell where an apple on a child's head was shot as a feat of expertise? Now imagine that the child is your customer, the apple his business and the archer (you) is blindfolded. What do you think would be the outcome of that exercise? Most likely, unless you are lucky, you will injure or kill the customer. You may think this is an extreme example but I would like to disagree. Most mediocre businesses operate this way, allowing their output to

17

change in ways which may certainly injure their customer's business. Always remember: **Your output is their input**. The hidden identity of this blindfolded archer is *variation*. In my book *The Flood, The Re-birth and The Race*, I describe the three stages which an organisation goes through on their journey to achieve customer happiness. Of all three stages, "The Flood" is the most affected by variation.

Variation can be natural or special. Both are a danger for the business but the latter is commonly known to cause more issues. I call variation "The Blindfolded Archer" because companies in "the Flood" stage have little control over the accuracy of their output and therefore being on target becomes more of a random event than a day-to-day given. Such companies shoot the arrow but have no certainty where it is going to land.

Variation, more than an enemy itself, is kind of the super power, the atomic bomb, if you wish, of all other enemies we will discuss in this book. The Blindfolded Archer is a sign of accumulated *points of failure* in your organisation, a sign of an illness that may kill your business if not treated promptly.

Working to defeat such enemies will allow your organisation to see clearly and therefore aim better.

THE
FORGOTTEN
LOVE
Your Second Enemy

We have all probably had a broken heart at some point in our lives, as somebody we love is not here anymore. Our relationship has ended. Sometimes this happens because we stop caring, or it may be the case that we care but we don't demonstrate it. Exactly the same thing happens in business. When we don't take the time to know our customers better, when we forget to talk to them continuously, to remind them how much we care, the relationship will end and some-body else will fill the gap.

If your business is designed properly, you will be focused on building a rela-tionship rather than only getting the money out of that single transaction. If designed properly, it will be a marriage, for life. A marriage based on that single most important asset we described ini-tially: Trust.

The Forgotten Love is a big enemy for obvious reasons, as it is your main asset that is taken away.

This enemy attacks by distracting your organisation with a smoke screen where the actions of the business are not aligned with either, A. What the cus-tomer knows they want or need now, or B. anticipating the needs of those same customers. In the latter, I am talking about your unique position to innovate and help them advance in their business.

Companies in "the Flood" stage can-not clearly see what is happening on the outside, and only begin to see on the oc-casion that something goes wrong. There is a complete disconnect from their cus-tomers and the relationship may only survive because they have an exclusivity contract or provide products or services which cannot be sourced anywhere else.

However, given the chance, their customers will run away as fast as they can.

THE UNQUALIFIED DRIVER
Your Third Enemy

Let me ask you a question: Would you lend your car to someone who you know for sure will crash it? Somebody who doesn't have the skills to take the car from A to B safely, along with its passengers? Your answer is most likely no. Now, let me ask you another one: Knowing from the first answer that you are concerned, would you take that person, sit down with them for 30 minutes, show them the basics and then give them the keys? The second is a better approach but yet, not good enough.

Even though we know that if some-one answered "yes" to both questions we would be appalled, the majority of Com-panies in "The Flood" and "The Rebirth" stages do it every day, and you probably do it as well. How many hours of training do you give to an employee to ensure he/she knows what needs to be done? And even if some training is done, do you make sure that the person understands and can do the job properly?

Don't get me wrong, I am not criticis-ing your organisation, all I want you to see here is one of the biggest enemies of excellence. The bigger your organisation is, the more systems you have. The less automated your business is, the more you rely on your employees to follow proce-dures, so the same outcome is achieved every time to avoid our Blindfolded Archer to enter the war. Finally, the more you have to rely on people, the more, and the better, training you must provide.

Many companies do a good job on re-cruiting good people but expect them to use their initiative to fill the existing gap due to poor training programs. These are more the type of companies in "The Re-birth" stage. Unfortunately, this comes at a great cost, not only to companies but also to customers because employees are left to learn by trial and error. This means that the speed of the organisation slows down and more mistakes are made.

Companies in "The Race" stage such as Disney, create a comprehensive program to ensure their employees are competent, and to ensure the best results right from the beginning. In the case of Disney University, the culture, rules, procedures, etc. are made clear, and competences are developed and evaluated.

Over the years, I have seen again and again how mistakes increase when temporary workers are hired to assist for a short period of time. This is a perfect example of an Unqualified Driver. On one hand, you have somebody who is not motivated to learn because they will just be there for a couple of months. On the other hand, the organisation may not be willing to use its resources to bring them up to speed.

The bigger the car, the more damage an Unqualified Driver can do. What I mean by this is that our enemy also attacks at the managerial level. This is where proper training systems are even scarcer because the higher you go, the less likely you are to find a "trainer to train the trainer." This particular type of driver has the keys to a gigantic truck and does their best to learn as fast as possible. Normally, they are more careful and methodical in the learning process, however, mistakes at a big scale can happen.

In our next example, we will learn about a killing machine which works in tandem with the Unqualified Driver to create a cycle of destruction.

THE ALZHEIMER'S SYNDROME
Your Fourth Enemy

This opponent has many weapons of its own and will use them all with no mercy.

As you already know, one of the most important assets for an organisation is the knowledge which allows them to make their product or service. This is a specialised knowledge which, if lost, will leave the organisation paralysed, incapable of achieving its target with confidence.

The Alzheimer's Syndrome starts its attack through the door which is left open by the Unqualified Driver. You see, with time, the Unqualified Driver will be in the position to train another driver. In this case, the former would have had time to learn more about their job and become more competent, however with a very big downside: They, by then, will have developed their own method and procedure. If everyone in the organisation does this, the business ends up with no standard way of making its products or services. Here is where our Blindfolded Archer gets their main source of power: Misalignment.

Our enemy, The Alzheimer's Syndrome, creates all this chaos by ensuring that every time knowledge is transferred from one person to another, it gets distorted, twisted, deformed, sometimes unrecognisably to the point where the business cannot make its products properly. This is evident in companies at the bottom of "The Flood" stage where the Alzheimer's Syndrome has conquered the land.

One of the weakest flanks our Alzheimer's Syndrome will always attack is that of customer requirements. If it manages to make the organisation forget them, he will have won the war. This is because, if a business is unclear about what the end goal is, what exactly its customer needs or expects, then there is no business.

Another strategy of this enemy is to attack at the edge, right where a section of the army finishes and another starts. It knows that it's right there, where communications can be cut to isolate its opponent, where the biggest damage can be caused. What I mean here is that in any business, communication is most likely to fail between departments. This results in only part of the critical information being provided, or no information at all, from one area to another.

This enemy affects the business in both the short and the long term. It robs your company of what I would say is the second most important asset: Its unique know-how.

POLICE
WITHOUT
GUNS
Your Fifth Enemy

What would happen in a society if people saw the police and they had no respect at all for them? If they didn't see a source of authority right there? There would be chaos, no enforcement, no peace, no security.

In exactly the same way, in the micro society that is your business, there must be a police department chasing and processing the particular type of criminals we are describing here. They say "Success leaves clues" and in the case of our 10 enemies, the clue to their achievements is one: **Errors.**

Many companies have a police department which is Quality, however, as sad as it is, the policemen working in such area have no guns. They are people with great intentions and knowledge but little or no power to process these business' enemies.

There are several common reasons for this. One of them is a conflict of interest. In many companies, the Quality head reports to the head of operations, meaning that the one accountable for the area where more mistakes are made, which directly affect customers, is the boss of the one fighting those mistakes. This doesn't sound that bad, however in companies in the "The Flood" stage where problems happen more often and in bigger sizes, it feels as if the boss of the police is the same boss of the gangsters. I say this because I have seen it. In my book *The Flood, The Rebirth and The Race*, Secret 5 explains the "Bypass Price Tag," as I call it, which is: Every operations director or manager will have a price tag to ignore mistakes in a product or service and will try to send it to its customers in the hopes that they don't notice. For some businesses, the price tag is 1,000, for others 100,000. The more compromised the business is due to a Quality issue, the more likely the boss of the Quality manager becomes both the boss of the police as well as the gangsters at the same time.

This is one of the reasons why Quality must report to the very top of the organisation so that there is no bias as to what action must be taken, no conflict of interest.

Now, that is only one source from which your Quality department gets its authority from, one of its guns if you will. The other one is the one that is conquered when a business manages to defeat the enemy we will be describing next.

THE BIG BROTHER'S SYNDROME
Your Sixth Enemy

When it comes to systems, centralisation is one of the best strategies for business success. However when it comes to people, it is one of the worst. The way this enemy attacks is by ensuring the organisation relies on one single person to make all the decisions regarding Quality, this is usually the Quality Manager. You know when this enemy is winning the battle because employees are not empowered to refuse orders that go against getting the best possible product out the door. You know it is wining when you have an organisation of followers with few leaders. Everyone looks at the Big Brother to solve their issues since they are unable to do it themselves. In an organisation in the "The Race" stage, 90 to 95% of the problems can be dealt with by the operative and mid-manager layers because they know exactly what needs to be achieved. In contrast, in companies in the "The Flood" stage, the Big Brother will be consulted about even the smallest decisions. Our Big Brother's Syndrome attack leaves behind a brain paralysis which can be lethal.

Our enemy's favourite tactic is to ensure the leaders of the organisation fall into this paralytic cycle, getting distracted from one of the most important activities they should not forget about: Replicating themselves to create soldiers to strengthen their army and win the war. Such replication is only possible by continuously getting your people to come up with solutions, not only questions. **Questions are great but solutions are king.**

Our Big Brother loves questions, but he runs away when soldiers start coming up with strategies of their own, creating an undefeatable army.

Picture your business as a single brain with two hands and two legs. A single human being. In the same way that our thinking and behaviour is a reflection of the people we interact with the most, the thinking and behaviour of an organisation is a reflection of all its members. Behaviour directly controls results. If the majority of the team have brain paralysis, the whole organisation will either stop or move very slowly. As a leader yourself, you cannot choose any of the two.

THE
GOLD
DIGGER
Your Seventh Enemy

This opponent in particular wants to steal the fortunes of the kingdom.

The wealth of an organisation comes in many different shapes such a customer trust, know-how, culture, and great team members, among others. Our opponent here is thirsty for a particular type: Time. The Gold Digger craves time because it is the prime raw material for a business to create the rest. Our Big Brother and our Gold Digger work very closely to ensure your business is handcuffed, immobilised.

Organisations in "The Flood" stage have no regard about the real value of time: They have long meetings without an agenda and no pre-established finish time. In this organisation, immediate response is expected for every request, destroying the plans, if any, made to achieve the important goals of the day. Employees in general are not able to quantitatively say if they had a good week or not.

Companies in "The Race" stage clearly understand the concept of *Environment for Success,* one where as many distractions as possible are removed because time is king. Companies which achieve Operational Excellence have won the battle against the Gold Digger, the battle of self-discipline and organisation discipline. If your company pays for 100% of the time the employee is there, then the team member should give 100% of their discipline to achieve the goal set.

The real size!

THE SURFACE SKIMMER
Your Eighth Enemy

This enemy operates very differently to the other opponents. It is actually the naval forces of our group of opponents. These naval forces have no submarines because they only operates on the surface. They stop you from submerging and let you see the real size of the iceberg floating on your waters.

The Surface Skimmer knows that by keeping you up there, it will allow all your other rivals to thrive, to steal your time, to forget, to paralyse your people, to stop you right in your tracks.

Companies in "The Flood" stage are notorious for operating this way: They will rarely try to find the real reason for a problem. They will only act if their business is at stake and, even then, they don't do a good job. They are just not qualified for deep water exploration.

The Surface Skimmer is a close ally of the Gold Digger. When organisations do not use every opportunity to look for points of failure, they will inevitably have to deal with the same problem again and again. Companies in "The Flood" stage choose to suffer their problems while companies in "The Race" choose to act. The ones in the latter recognise that it is not possible to fix all problems at once and therefore they create systems to prioritise and take focused action.

The surface Skimmer whispers in the ear of its opponent, "You are too busy, you have so much going on. If they want you to submerge they need someone else to take your load." Mediocre organisations love this motto because it is a way of procrastinating, of justifying no action without feeling bad.

THE
SELF-DESTRUCTION
BUTTON
Your Ninth Enemy

The bigger your company is, the more likely it is to push such button. Why? Because the bigger and more complex, the more difficult it is for its team members to see the consequences of their actions.

In the same way a building is demolished to make room for a new, bigger, better, improved one, companies are continuously destroyed as improvement is introduced. You see, everyone talks about it, craves it, but few people understand that improvement is a double edged sword: If it is not done carefully, you will end up with more, and bigger, problems than you started with.

The Self-Destruction Button is pushed every time something is changed without assessing first what other parts of your system are connected to it, what parts will stop working once we introduce the modification. Our enemy very much enjoys every time the change happens on a supporting beam of a critical system because the whole process may just collapse in a symphony of dust, metal and gravel. Sometimes it is a recall, sometimes a lawsuit. Fortunately, most of the time it just means reworking and additional changes.

Companies in "The Race" stage understand clearly the "*Controlled Innovation*" concept. I define this concept as "*encouraging innovation at all levels but using clear rules for its introduction into existing systems to avoid negative effects.*" In other words, improvement is necessary, but should not be done by amateurs, by Unqualified Drivers.

THE UNWILLING SPY

Your Tenth Enemy

We have talked about him before when discussing our Police Without Guns opponent. The rival could easily be yourself. Yes, the leader of your organisation.

The reason you may be an Unwilling Spy is because when you allow any of the other enemies to constantly operate, to constantly attack the protective walls of the castle, let alone let them in, you find yourself working as a double spy. Most business leaders I know are hardworking, intelligent people but the issue is that intelligence does not make up for ignorance. Therefore, your organisation must be constantly acquiring the right knowledge so that they can make the right decisions in order to create the right culture. This results in new leaders being discovered and groomed, your police department getting the authority and impartiality required, and time being used wisely to increase the wealth stored in the vault of the fortress.

Now that you can recognise your enemies clearly, let's learn about the weapons you can use to win the war.

THE 5 PILLARS OF OPERATIONAL EXCELLENCE

Operational Excellence has one single goal: To achieve to meet customer requirements, which is a big part of customer happiness. Operational excellence can only be achieved through accuracy, and accuracy brings to the table a precious asset for achievement, which is clarity. That is what our first two pillars are about.

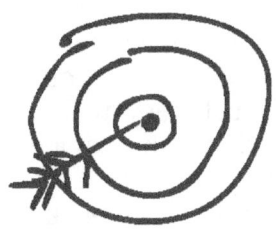

EXTERNAL
CLARITY
First Pillar

This building pillar is about the information we provide to our customers and what that information comes back as.

Let me explain, in order to get new customers, all businesses make promises of what they can deliver so that they can create the trust we have already discussed. Such promises will then be combined with customer's specific expectations, in the first and any subsequent orders that they may place. For example, you may promise delivery of hot pizza in less than 30 minutes, as Domino's Pizza did during its beginning. This promise may return as an order where a customer expects a 30 minute or less delivery time of hot and fresh food with great customer service, and if there are any problems, they expect to get their money refunded with no effort. Now that you have built some initial trust, they will continue to order, but only if you provide the same performance (no mistakes) every time. I have used a simple example here, but the key is that your business must make a continuous effort to collect every single expectation of that customer and make sure that it is clearly communicated to all departments which participate in activities towards meeting such expectations. These expectations come in two forms. The first type is the ones that will be explicitly communicated such as delivery date, amount, and colour, etc. The second type are expectations which a customer won't state but that need to be met such as delivery integrity, general presentation, packaging configuration, etc. In the non-stated ones, some are what you would call common sense ones and others are internal, which lead to, for example, the delivery integrity discussed. Wherever they come from, there must be an effort to collect them and define them clearly.

Clear definition means being able to measure them, otherwise your business ends up with vague requirements which you won't be able to enforce. Sometimes, it is very difficult to define such requirements, let alone measure them. An example that illustrates this point happens in the aromas industry where defining the aroma profile of a sample is extremely difficult. I used to do consultancy for a company which traded with such materials, and we had to find cutting edge technology to precisely define the requirement for such components. It was the only way to ensure consistency: Clarity in customer requirements.

Requirements from customers change and, therefore, your business must have a system to have those up to date.

Making sure requirements are written down ensures that they are not just stored in people's heads where our enemy, The Alzheimer's Syndrome, can attack.

There must also be clarity in terms of promising only what the business has capacity to deliver. Otherwise, current and future customers will be undoubtedly disappointed. Sales people tend to exaggerate what the company can do just to get the sale, however, this is a disrespect to the relationship we want to build with customers because it is known beforehand that the business won't be able to deliver what was promised.

Operational Excellence is defined as conformance to requirements. Therefore, having clarity on what your end user requires will take you a step closer to customer happiness, to "The Race" stage.

INTERNAL CLARITY

Second Pillar

In our first pillar, we described how you must achieve clarity in all exchanges of information that go out and come back from your customers. Now, the second pillar tells us that such clarity must also be internal. Something very important to note here is that when I talk about clarity, I am also referring to accuracy combined with efficiency. Why? Because we all, as customers, want everything delivered with no mistakes and on time. In other words, we want no errors and no delays.

For a company to achieve the kind of operational excellence that will take it to "The Race" stage, it is necessary to make a continuous effort to remove points of failure in all processes where information is likely to break. You see, Quality in any company works like a relay race: Every department hands off the baton to the next one, so the race can be completed. In our case, the difference is that the baton contains information which must not lose its integrity as it goes from unit to unit.

Internal clarity must be focused on two main areas. The first is getting the organisation to understand that the ultimate goal of Zero Errors is what we all, as customers, have in our minds. The second is that the Zero Errors performance, from a customer point of view, is simply expected; it is a baseline, a given. So, at the same time that everyone works to achieve operational excellence, they must also work to "wow" the customer, to surprise them, to give added value. Walt Disney understood this very well and he used to refer to it as "The Whole Package." I call it a "Total Solution." I describe this in more detail in my book *Customer Happyland*.

ACCURATE
KNOWLEDGE
Third Pillar

A company won't be able to achieve Zero Errors unless the knowledge required to make physical goods, or to produce a required service, leads to consistency. This is the opposite of our Blindfolded Archer enemy's effect.

Companies in "The Race" stage make a big effort to introduce as much automation as possible. The reason is that automation removes "operative decision making" which is nothing more than the so famous human error. In order to develop systems (and automate them), the necessary knowledge must be gathered, simplified and streamlined. However, this unavoidably leads companies to extract the critical knowledge from the minds of its team members. This process leads to incredible gains in efficiency and accuracy because the new system guides and controls the behaviour of its users.

Accurate knowledge also means that such know-how must be shared so it is available when needed, without losing integrity.

Knowledge is always changing: It is destroyed by being improved on or by being forgotten (think of our Self-Destruction Button). That is why, apart from continuously working on improving knowledge accuracy, the organisation must create a culture of capturing and introducing the new know-how formally so it outlasts time and people.

EDUCATION
Fourth Pillar

Let me ask you a question: Of what use is a book you buy but leave on the shelf to gather dust? Well, not much apart from the fact that it is there to remind you it must be read. In the same way, if knowledge in a company is available (think written manuals, procedures, etc.) but there is not a structure by which people are educated and the transfer of such knowledge is not properly evaluated to determine if the process was effective, then there is no point. Mistakes will be made regardless.

Companies in "The Race" stage have strong educational systems which lead to consistency. As I mentioned before, Disney has the Disney University. Zappos, a shoe retailer, gives four weeks of employee training on customer service to every team member in the company. The Container Store, a retailer specialised in selling items to better organise your home or office, provides its personnel with ten times more training than the average business in retail. What is the result of this? All three companies are among the best organisations in the world because they achieve accuracy, efficiency and customer happiness. They are prepared to provide a Total Solution.

Many companies fool themselves by bringing in only external training, leaving the internal one to chance. The reason for this is partly ignorance of the pillars we have discussed here, but mostly due to something that happens in every business: All managers are *so busy being busy*. As a result of this, they do not allocate time for one of the most critical activities in any business, which is the continuous education of team members. At the Container Store, full time employees receive 263 hours of training which is what they call "Foundation Training." Furthermore, new managers get additional training which is described by the company as such: "*In addition to Foundation Training, a new store manager completes five additional weeks of training to cover topics such as Leadership, People, Operations and Running the Business.*" Can you tell how many hours your training system contains?

Smart companies work to build this pillar from the strongest material so the knowledge is where it is needed, when it is needed.

RISK REMOVAL
Fifth Pillar

In terms of personal development, there is no growth if there is no self-analysis. If a person cannot say where his actions are causing reactions opposite to what is intended, be it unconsciously or intentionally, there won't be improvement. An organisation is no different.

This pillar is critical and fights back directly to our Surface Skimmer opponent. Albert Einstein's definition of insanity was: "*Doing the same thing over and over again and expecting different results.*" If we apply this to your business, I would say that: An insane organisation is one that wants to achieve excellence by making the same mistakes over and over. This is also related to GE former CEO, Jack Welsh, who used to say: *"Making a mistake is not a problem, the problem is making such a mistake more than once."*

A good indication of how much Risk Removal work your organisation does is by first having a look at your last month and trying to determine what percentage of your time you were working on fixing errors. After that, have a look at what percentage you were working on improving systems to avoid errors. Finally, find out what percentage you spent optimising existing processes to make the business more efficient. If you take the time to do that, you will effectively be looking at how much you were working on the past, the present and the future of your organisation. In turn, this will give you a very good indication of whether your business is in the Flood, The Rebirth or the Race stage. Companies in "The Flood" stage are the worst at risk removal. Where is your company at the moment?

Risk Removal is about looking at the future, about not waiting for the problems to appear but to foresee them through self-analysis and remove them.

This is a lot more difficult than investigating a problem after it has already happened but, then again, it is a lot more profitable.

A company in "The Race" stage looks at the future via innovation to strengthen its systems by simplification, streamlining, error proofing, automation, training and so on. All of this is aimed at giving customers a unique service which they will rave about.

CONCLUSION

We have discussed the 10 enemies of operational excellence and our 5 weapons to defeat them. By now, you should have a clearer picture of what needs to be done on a global basis to align your business in the direction your customer needs you to.

Make no mistake, this is not an easy exercise, but one that needs to be done. Is your organisation an insane one? Which stage are you at the moment? Are you putting the resources where they need to be? Are you developing the right habits to get to and conquer Customer Happyland? As a leader of your organisation, you must be able to answer those questions or, at the very least, be actively exploring the answers.

Join my community to help you answer such questions.

If you want to get an initial score to determine how strong your operations are, please go to to download your "Operational Excellence Score" tool.

www.noelcardona.com/opex

I am here to help you accelerate your journey towards customer happiness: **Operational excellence is just a milestone on such journey.**

Thank you for your time, and congratulations again for making it this far as it shows you can allocate time and finish what you started - Exactly as it needs to be in any business.